DISCOVER&
LEARN

CONTINENTS & OCEANS

by
Charlie Ogden

Photo Credits

Abbreviations: l-left, r-right, b-bottom, t-top, c-centre, m-middle, lo-lower, up-upper.

Front Cover – capitanoseye. 2 – NIKKOS DESKALAKIS. 4t – Taiga. 4tm – Insta_photos. 4b – Lewis Tse Pui Lung. 5t – In Green. 5m – Viacheslav Lopatin. 5b – Matteo Valpone. 6m – Creative Travel Projects. 6b – duchy. 7t – f11photo. 7b – Robert Hoetink. 8m – Artush. 8b – Martin Macnarowski. 9t – Origomisan Ogbebor. 9bl – Kojin. 9bm – Cathy Keifer. 9br - angelo lano. 10 – Seqoya. 11tl – Anastasios71. 11tm – S.Borisov. 11tr – ESB Professional. 11b – Emi Cristea. 12t – Filip Fuxa. 12m – Lucky-photographer. 12b – Gail Johnson. 13t – sumikophoto. 13b – Diego Grandi. 14t – nattanan726. 14m – Jess Kraft. 14b – ostill. 15t – VadimPetraov. 15b – mezzotint. 16bl – Luke Shelley. 16bm – Urban Napflin. – 16br – rickyd. 17t – ChameleionsEye. 17m – Sara Winter. 17b – Ruth Lawton. 18tl – axily. 18m – Li Hui Chen. 18b – Willem Tims. 19t – axily. 19m – Shay Yacobinski. 19b – Vadim Sadovski. 20m – Rich Carey. 20b – Hanimo. 21t – Ethan Daniels. 21upm – Sean Pavone. 21lom – DJG. 21b – c.mokri – austria. 22 – CHEN WS. 23t – Sergejus Lamanosovas. 23b – LaMiaFotografia. 24m – Pabkov. 24b – Igor Grochev. 25ml - Khoroshunova Olga. 25mr – Stockimo. 25b – Rajarshi Bhattacharya. 27m – Catmando. 27lom – fotorequest. 27lom – Vladimir Melnik. 27bl – bikeriderlondon. 27bm – Smit. 27br – Moverton. 28bl – Anton_Ivanov. 28bm – By damerau. 28br – Ethan Daniels. 29bl ohrim. 29bm – MrPhotoMania. 29br – Claudiowl. 30ml – Balu. 30m – Dudarev Mikhail. 30mr – The Clay Machine Gun. 30b -Anton Balazh. Images are courtesy of Shutterstock.com. With thanks to Getty Images, Thinkstock Photo and iStockphoto.

BookLife
PUBLISHING

©2020
BookLife Publishing Ltd.
King's Lynn
Norfolk PE30 4LS

ISBN: 978-1-83927-821-1

Written by:
Charlie Ogden

Edited by:
Holly Duhig

Designed by:
Gareth Liddington

All rights reserved.
Printed in Malaysia.

A catalogue record for this book
is available from the British Library.

All facts, statistics, web addresses and URLs in this book were verified as valid and accurate at time of writing. No responsibility for any changes to external websites or references can be accepted by either the author or publisher.

CONTENTS

Words in **bold** are explained in the glossary on page 31.

CONTINENTS
AND OCEANS

The surface of the Earth is made up of land and water. The land can be split up into seven continents that together contain snow-capped mountains, wild jungles and thousands of unique **cultures**. The water covers over 70 percent (%) of Earth's surface and can be broken down into five giant oceans.

Arctic Ocean

North America

Atlantic Ocean

Europe

Asia

Africa

Pacific Ocean

South America

Indian Ocean

Australia

Southern Ocean

Antarctica

OCEANS

Not all the water on Earth is found in the five oceans. Outside of these main oceans, there are also a number of smaller areas of water called seas. For example, there is the Mediterranean Sea and the Caribbean Sea.

CARIBBEAN SEA

MEDITERRANEAN SEA

CONTINENTS

The land on Earth is broken up into seven continents; Africa, Asia, North America, South America, Europe, Australia and Antarctica. Each of these continents is mostly made up of one large piece of land. However, continents can also include a number of nearby **islands**.

ZANZIBAR IS AN ISLAND OFF THE EAST COAST OF AFRICA. IT IS PART OF AFRICA EVEN THOUGH IT ISN'T CONNECTED TO THE AFRICAN **MAINLAND**.

Continents are made up of lots of **countries**. Most countries are only part of one continent, but a select few are part of two continents. Countries vary in size a lot – some countries are very small and some are very big. The smallest country in the world is Vatican City, which is in Europe. The largest country in the world is Russia, which is in Europe and Asia.

MOSCOW, RUSSIA

VATICAN CITY

ASIA

Asia is the largest continent on Earth as well as the continent with the highest **population**. Over 4.4 billion people live in Asia.

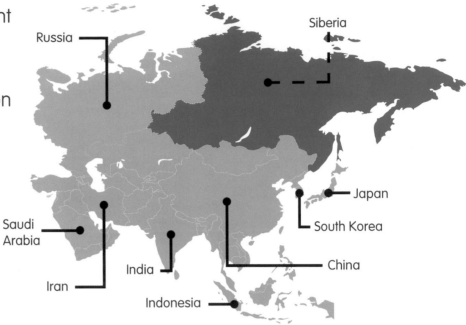

Russia

Siberia

Saudi Arabia

Iran

India

Indonesia

China

Japan

South Korea

As Asia is so large, it shouldn't be a surprise that it has a huge range of different **landscapes**. In northern areas, such as Siberia, the winters are long and very cold. However, countries in southeast Asia, such as Indonesia, have a tropical climate and are warm for most of the year.

Siberia makes up nearly 10% of all the land on Earth.

SIBERIA

LOMBOK, INDONESIA

Asia is home to some of the biggest cities in the world. Tokyo, the capital city of Japan, is the largest city in Asia. It is home to over 37 million people, which is around the same as the entire population for the country of Canada.

TOKYO, JAPAN

Asia was home to many of the first human **civilisations**. Over 10,000 years ago, small groups of people began to make their homes in an area of Asia that is now the countries of Iraq, Iran and Syria. This area is sometimes called the Fertile Crescent because the soil there was very **fertile** compared to surrounding areas.

Iraq

Syria

Fertile Crescent

Iran

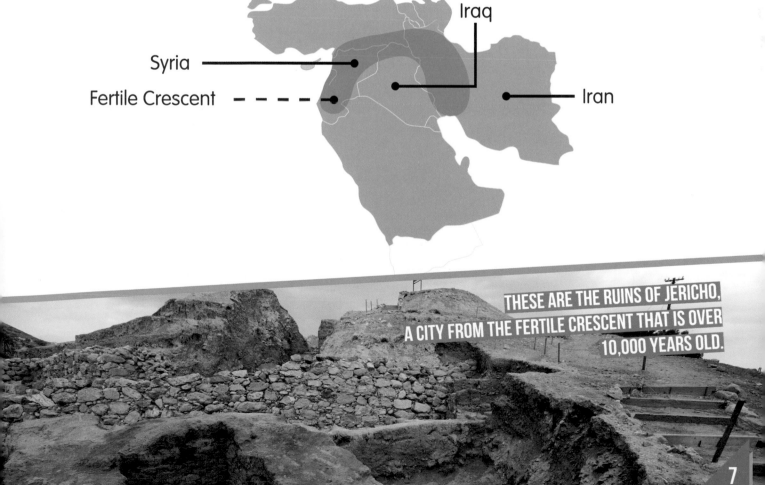

THESE ARE THE RUINS OF JERICHO, A CITY FROM THE FERTILE CRESCENT THAT IS OVER 10,000 YEARS OLD.

AFRICA

Africa is the second-largest continent and it is home to over 1.2 billion people.

The majority of Africa receives hot weather all year round. In hot and dry parts of Africa there are often large, sandy deserts. In hot and wet areas of Africa there are huge rainforests that are home to gorillas, elephants and monkeys.

Morocco

Egypt

Ethiopia

Nigeria

Uganda

Namibia

Madagascar

South Africa

THE NAMIB DESERT IN NAMIBIA, AFRICA

The Virunga Mountains in Africa are one of the only places in the world where mountain gorillas live.

THE VIRUNGA MOUNTAINS IN UGANDA, AFRICA

There are probably more individual cultures in Africa than any other continent on Earth. Africa is home to many countries that each have their own cultures. It is thought that there are around 3,000 different languages in Africa.

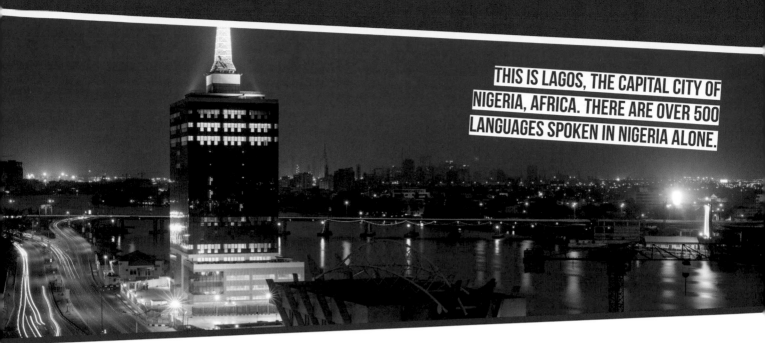

THIS IS LAGOS, THE CAPITAL CITY OF NIGERIA, AFRICA. THERE ARE OVER 500 LANGUAGES SPOKEN IN NIGERIA ALONE.

One of the biggest islands in the world, Madagascar, is part of Africa. Madagascar is home to many **species** of animals and plants that cannot be found anywhere else in the world, including lemurs, chameleons and baobab trees.

PANTHER CHAMELEON

RING-TAILED LEMUR

BAOBAB TREES

EUROPE

Europe is the third-most populated continent after Asia and Africa. Europe is connected to Asia and is a part of the same **landmass**, which is known as Eurasia.

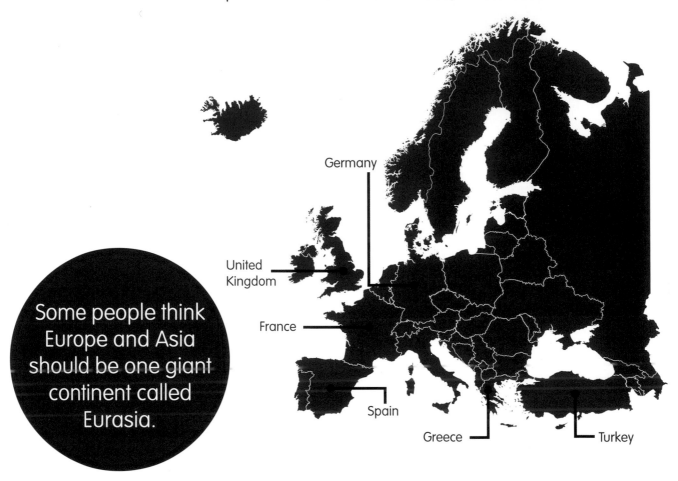

Germany

United Kingdom

France

Spain

Greece

Turkey

Some people think Europe and Asia should be one giant continent called Eurasia.

Even though Europe is the third-most populated continent, it is one of the smallest in size at just over 10,000 square kilometres. Only the continent of Australia is smaller than it in size.

THIS IS ISTANBUL, THE LARGEST CITY IN TURKEY. PART OF IT IS IN ASIA AND THE OTHER PART IS IN EUROPE.

Over the centuries, Europe has been home to many of the world's most powerful and beautiful cities. It is also home to some of the world's oldest cities.

ATHENS, THE CAPITAL CITY OF GREECE, WAS FOUNDED OVER 5,000 YEARS AGO.

ROME, THE CAPITAL CITY OF ITALY, WAS FOUNDED OVER 2,500 YEARS AGO.

LONDON, THE CAPITAL CITY OF ENGLAND, WAS FOUNDED AROUND 2,000 YEARS AGO.

Many of the oldest cities in Europe were founded by the ancient Greeks or the ancient Romans – two of the most important and powerful civilisations to ever exist. These two civilisations made huge advances in areas such as mathematics, medicine, **politics** and science. People all around the world still benefit from the advances made by these two ancient European civilisations.

THIS IS THE TEMPLE OF CONCORDIA IN SICILY, ITALY. IT WAS BUILT BY THE ANCIENT GREEKS NEARLY 2,500 YEARS AGO.

NORTH AMERICA

North America is the third-largest continent after Asia and Africa and it is home to over 550 million people.

Unlike most continents, the majority of North America is made up of only two countries. The United States and Canada, together, take up most of the land on the North American continent.

Greenland

Canada

United States of America

Cuba

Caribbean Islands

Mexico

Guatemala

Panama

There are lots of islands that also make up part of North America. Many of these islands are in the Caribbean Sea and are also part of North America.

BARBADOS

JAMAICA

There are over 7,000 islands in the Caribbean.

CUBA

North America is home to some of the world's most amazing natural wonders. The Grand Canyon is one of the biggest **canyons** in the world. It was carved out of the rock over millions of years by the powerful Colorado River.

THE GRAND CANYON, ARIZONA, US

The ruins of many ancient cities can also be found in North America. Most of these cities belonged to the Mayan civilisation, which began in North America around 2000 BC and lasted for over 3,500 years. One of the most well-preserved Mayan ruins is the ancient city of Tikal in the jungles of Guatemala.

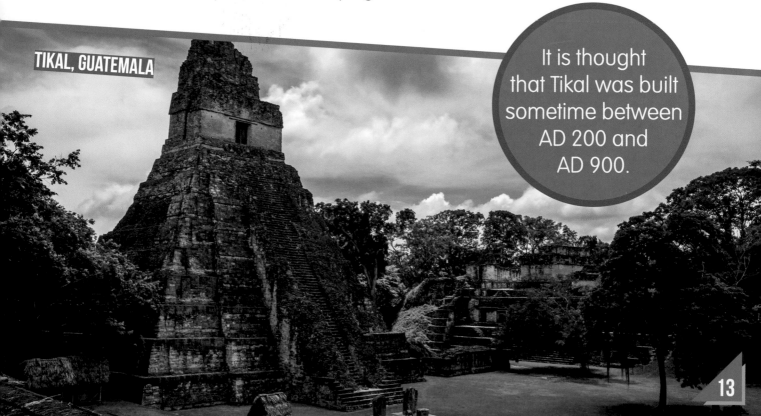

TIKAL, GUATEMALA

It is thought that Tikal was built sometime between AD 200 and AD 900.

SOUTH AMERICA

South America is the fourth-largest continent and it is home to over 400 million people.

South America is home to the biggest rainforest in the world, the Amazon rainforest. The rainforest stretches over nine countries and is home to the Amazon River, which is one of the longest rivers in the world. Many amazing animals live in this rainforest, including monkeys, sloths and jaguars.

Colombia

Venezuela

Amazon Rainforest

Peru

Bolivia

Brazil

Argentina

BROWN-THROATED SLOTH

HOWLER MONKEY

JAGUAR

There are still small tribes living in the Amazon rainforest that have had no contact with the rest of the world.

The Amazon rainforest is so amazing that people often overlook the many other natural wonders in South America, such as the mountain landscapes and dry, dusty deserts.

The Andes mountain range, which runs through seven different countries, is the longest on-land mountain range in the world. It is around 7,000 kilometres long and is home to both giant mountains and fiery volcanoes.

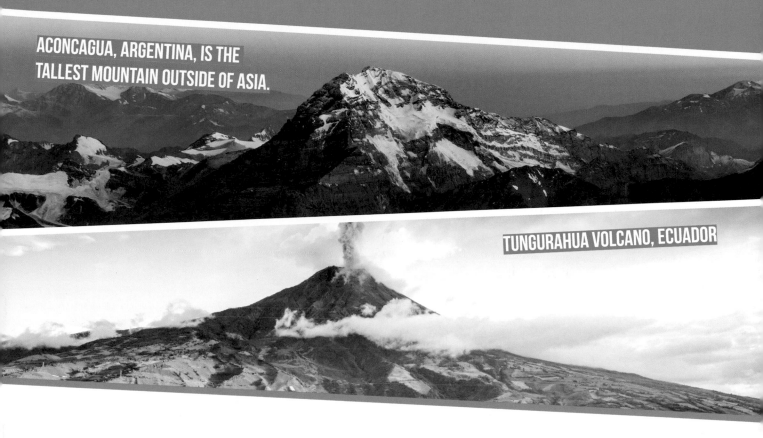

ACONCAGUA, ARGENTINA, IS THE TALLEST MOUNTAIN OUTSIDE OF ASIA.

TUNGURAHUA VOLCANO, ECUADOR

The Atacama Desert, which stretches across the South American countries of Chile, Peru, Bolivia and Argentina, is one of the driest and flattest places on Earth. Most creatures find it very hard to live in the Atacama Desert, but one creature that manages to thrive here is the flamingo.

ATACAMA DESERT, BOLIVIA

AUSTRALIA

The smallest and second-least populated continent in the world is Australia. The continent of Australia contains the country of Australia as well as a number of other countries. The term 'Oceania' is used to refer to a region that includes the Australian continent plus some nearby islands that aren't a part of any continent, such as New Zealand.

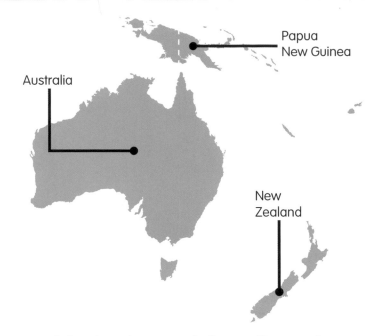

Papua New Guinea

Australia

New Zealand

Australia has been separate from the rest of the land on Earth for millions of years. Because of this, there are many weird and wonderful animals that only live on the Australian continent and its surrounding islands. These include kangaroos, kiwi birds and koalas.

KANGAROO

KIWI

KOALA

The Australian continent has been separated from the other land on Earth for over 100 million years.

The **indigenous** people of Australia and its surrounding islands have very rich and interesting cultures that are known around the world. The indigenous people of Australia are called Aboriginal Australians. Amongst other things, they are known for inventing the didgeridoo – a long, cylindrical musical instrument.

DIDGERIDOO

For many years, people in Europe were unaware that Australia existed. The first European to land on the Australian mainland was Willem Janszoon on the 26th of February, 1606. He named the place where he landed New Zeeland after an area of the Netherlands called Zeeland. The name New Zealand is now used for an island to the southeast of Australia, which was discovered by Europeans around 40 years later.

AUSTRALIA

NEW ZEALAND

The famous explorer Captain James Cook didn't land on Australia until 1770, 164 years after Willem Janszoon.

ANTARCTICA

The last continent on Earth is Antarctica. Antarctica is the farthest south of all the continents and it is home to the South Pole. It is the coldest and windiest continent in the world.

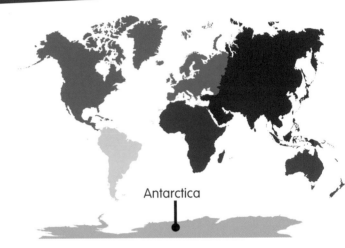

Antarctica

There are no countries in Antarctica and the conditions are too hostile for anyone to want to live there all the time. During the summer months, around 4,000 people may be living in Antarctica at any one time. Most of these people are scientists who stay in Antarctica to do experiments.

The coldest temperature ever recorded on Earth was -97.8°C at Vostok Research Station in Antarctica.

THIS IS A RESEARCH STATION AT PORT LOCKROY, ANTARCTICA.

The distance between Antarctica and South America is around 800 kilometres. This is the shortest distance between Antarctica and another continent. As well as this, the ocean that surrounds Antarctica is covered in large chunks of sea ice for most of the year. This makes it very difficult to get to Antarctica.

Humans had sailed boats around most the world and discovered most of the planets in our solar system before anyone had ever heard of or seen Antarctica. It was found in 1820, when a Russian boat came across it by accident. It is thought that in 1821, John Davis became the first person to set foot in Antarctica. Antarctica's sea ice and **remote** location made it one of the most difficult continents to explore.

NEW ZEALAND WAS ONE OF THE LAST ISLANDS TO BE DISCOVERED. HOWEVER, IT WAS FIRST SETTLED ON AROUND AD 1250 – OVER 500 YEARS BEFORE ANTARCTICA WAS DISCOVERED.

ASTRONOMERS KNEW ABOUT JUPITER AND MANY OTHER PLANETS IN THE SOLAR SYSTEM MANY YEARS BEFORE ANTARCTICA WAS DISCOVERED.

PACIFIC OCEAN

The Pacific Ocean is the largest of Earth's five oceans and it covers around one-third of the planet's surface. It stretches all the way from the Arctic Ocean in the north to the Southern Ocean in the south. It is **bordered** by North America, South America, Asia and Australia.

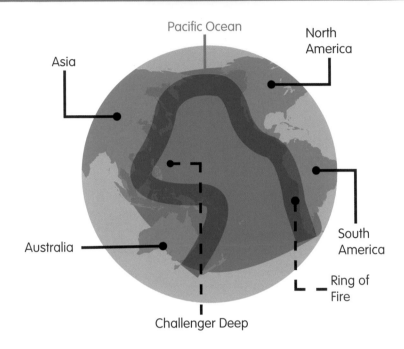

Pacific Ocean

Asia

North America

Australia

South America

Ring of Fire

Challenger Deep

The Pacific Ocean is home to the deepest point on the planet – Challenger Deep in the Mariana Trench. The Mariana Trench was made when two parts of Earth's outer crust, known as **tectonic plates**, moved away from each other, leaving a trench between them. The deepest part of the trench, known as Challenger Deep, goes down 10,911 metres below the surface of the water. If you put 24 Empire State Buildings into the trench, one on top of the other, they still wouldn't be tall enough to reach the ocean's surface.

Only three people have been near the bottom of Challenger Deep. That's fewer people than have walked on the Moon!

THE MARIANA TRENCH IS NAMED AFTER THE NEARBY MARIANA ISLANDS IN THE PACIFIC OCEAN.

As the Pacific Ocean is the deepest ocean in the world, it is home to many creatures that do not live anywhere else on Earth. These creatures live down in the dark depths of the Pacific Ocean where the **pressure** is very high. If these creatures swam in shallower waters with less pressure, they would die.

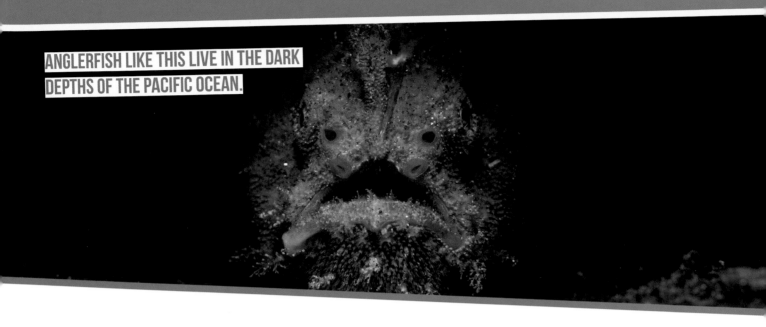

ANGLERFISH LIKE THIS LIVE IN THE DARK DEPTHS OF THE PACIFIC OCEAN.

The Pacific Ocean is also home to the Ring of Fire, a huge belt of underwater and on-land volcanoes that surrounds most of the ocean. It begins around New Zealand, moves up the east coast of Asia, continues across to North America and then goes all the way down the west coast of South America.

MT. FUJI, JAPAN

MOUNT ST HELENS

All of these volcanoes are part of the Ring of Fire.

PARINACOTA, BOLIVIA

ATLANTIC OCEAN

The Atlantic Ocean is the second-largest ocean after the Pacific Ocean and it covers around 20% of the Earth's surface. It stretches from the Arctic Ocean in the north to the Southern Ocean in the south. It is surrounded by North America, South America, Europe and Africa.

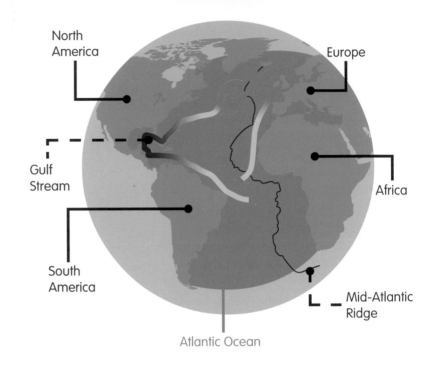

North America

Europe

Gulf Stream

Africa

South America

Mid-Atlantic Ridge

Atlantic Ocean

The Atlantic Ocean is home to the longest mountain range in the world, the Mid-Atlantic Ridge. This mountain range was created by the tectonic plates in Europe and Africa moving away from the tectonic plates in North America and South America. As the plates spread apart, **magma** from inside the Earth shot out, cooled and formed the mountain range.

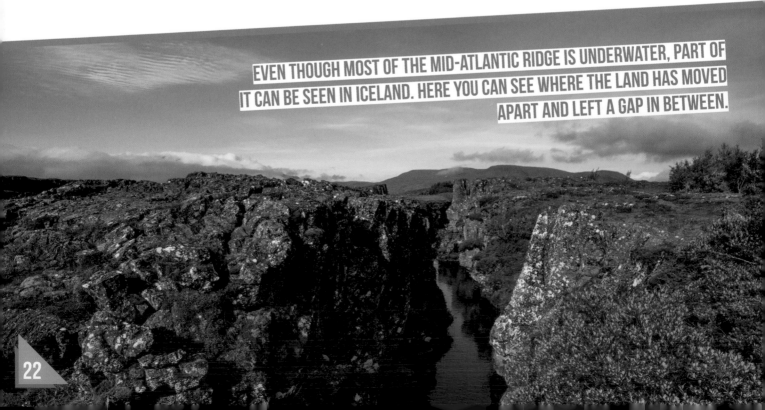

EVEN THOUGH MOST OF THE MID-ATLANTIC RIDGE IS UNDERWATER, PART OF IT CAN BE SEEN IN ICELAND. HERE YOU CAN SEE WHERE THE LAND HAS MOVED APART AND LEFT A GAP IN BETWEEN.

Even though oceans are large, single bodies of water, they often contain large streams of water that move in very specific directions. These are called ocean currents and they can have a huge effect on their surrounding area.

ISLE OF SKYE, INNER HEBRIDES, SCOTLAND

The Gulf Stream is an ocean current in the Atlantic Ocean. Water off the west coast of Africa is moved by the ocean current into the Gulf of Mexico, which is where the Gulf Stream gets its name. Here, the water is heated by the Sun before moving onto Greenland, Iceland, northern Europe and northwest Africa.

LOFOTEN, NORWAY

The warm water that moves through the Gulf Stream helps to give nearby areas a warmer climate. This effect is most noticeable on the Scottish islands and on Norway's coast. Were it not for the Gulf Stream, these places would be a lot colder and would be covered in snow for much of the year.

INDIAN OCEAN

The Indian Ocean is the third-largest ocean in the world. It is also the warmest ocean in the world, which is why many people visit islands in the Indian Ocean for their holidays. It is bordered by Africa to the west, Asia to the north and Australia to the east.

The Indian Ocean is one of the busiest oceans. Ships of all kinds move through this ocean, transporting goods between Africa, the Middle East, Europe, India, China and Southeast Asia. The Suez Canal, which is an important **canal** that connects the Indian Ocean to the Mediterranean Sea, allows ships to move between Europe and the Indian Ocean without having to sail around Africa.

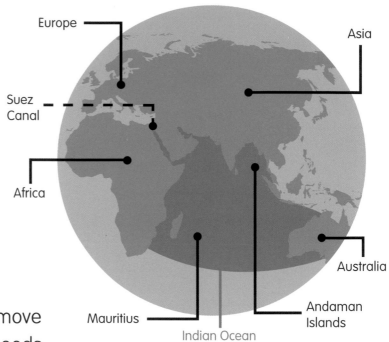

Europe

Asia

Suez Canal

Africa

Mauritius

Indian Ocean

Andaman Islands

Australia

SUEZ CANAL, EGYPT

The Suez Canal separates Asia from Africa by just a 200-metre-wide strip of water.

Many of the world's most beautiful, tropical and intriguing islands are found scattered around the Indian Ocean. One of the most notable of these islands is Mauritius. Today, many people spend their holidays on this island enjoying its beaches and warm climate. However, until 1681 it was the only place on Earth where one particular species of dodo bird lived.

MAURITIUS

THIS IS WHAT THE DODO BIRD USED TO LOOK LIKE.

Humans hunted the dodo bird until it went **extinct**. Nowadays, the dodo is used as a symbol to show the damage that humans can do to nature.

The Indian Ocean is also home to one of the last uncontacted tribes outside of the Amazon rainforest. North Sentinel Island in the Andaman Islands – a group of islands between India and Southeast Asia – is the home of the Sentinelese people. The Sentinelese people are a tribe of up to 500 people that have remained uncontacted by modern civilisations. Many people believe that the Sentinelese people do not know how to farm or make fire.

JOLLY BUOY ISLAND, ANDAMAN ISLANDS

ARCTIC OCEAN

The Arctic Ocean is the smallest, shallowest and farthest north of all the world's oceans. The ocean is almost completely covered in ice during winter and borders the continents of North America, Europe and Asia. It is also home to the North Pole.

Because the climate is so cold, large sections of the Arctic Ocean are frozen all year round. This makes it possible to reach the North Pole, the northernmost point on the planet, on foot. By 1910, many people had claimed to have reached the North Pole on foot. However, all of these claims are disputed and their truth is hard to prove.

North America

Arctic Ocean

Asia

North Pole

Europe

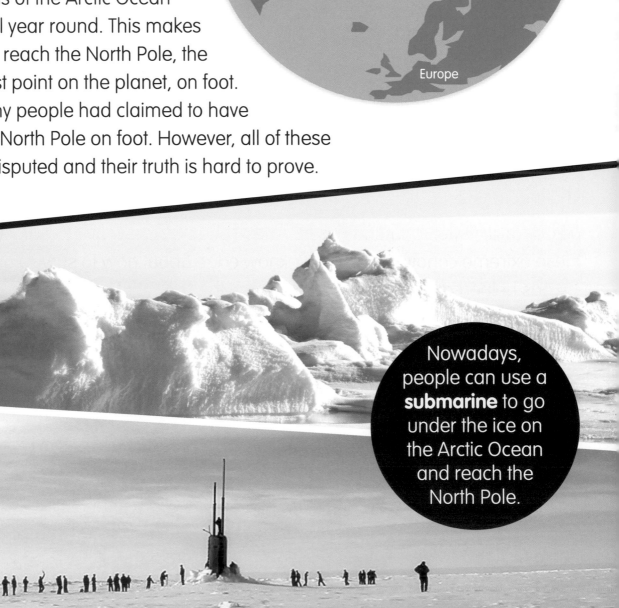

Nowadays, people can use a **submarine** to go under the ice on the Arctic Ocean and reach the North Pole.

The animals that live in the Arctic Ocean – or on top of its frozen surface – are some of the toughest animals in the world. They deal with constant freezing temperatures and food can often be hard to find. Along with polar bears and sled dogs, this part of the world is home to orcas, snowy owls and walruses.

ORCAS

SNOWY OWL

WALRUS

However, these creatures aren't the only ones that live in this part of the world. Inuits and other groups of people live in Arctic areas near the Arctic Ocean such as Canada, Greenland and Russia. These people have learnt how to survive in these extreme conditions and their knowledge about how to survive on the sea ice has helped many **expeditions** to reach the North Pole.

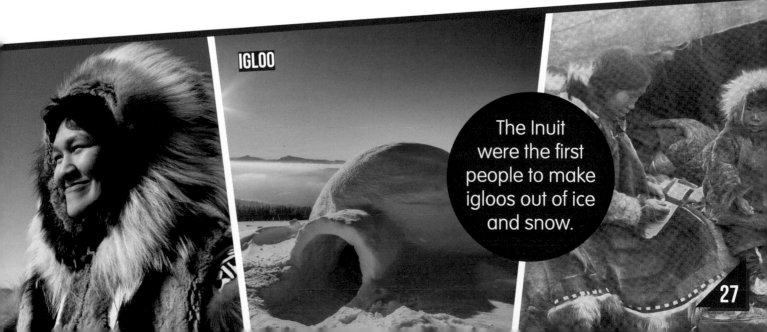

IGLOO

The Inuit were the first people to make igloos out of ice and snow.

SOUTHERN OCEAN

The Southern Ocean is the second-smallest ocean in the world after the Arctic Ocean. The Southern Ocean completely surrounds the continent of Antarctica.

Many people have argued that there is no Southern Ocean and that the waters around Antarctica should be considered to be part of the Atlantic, Pacific and Indian oceans instead. However, the cold climate and the Antarctic ice makes the water in the Southern Ocean very different to that in the surrounding oceans. The water in the Southern Ocean moves eastward around Antarctica in the world's longest ocean current.

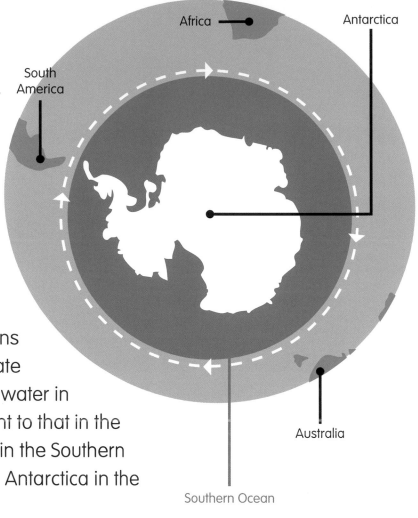

Africa

Antarctica

South America

Australia

Southern Ocean

There are many icebergs in the Southern Ocean, which makes it a very dangerous ocean to sail.

WORLD OCEAN

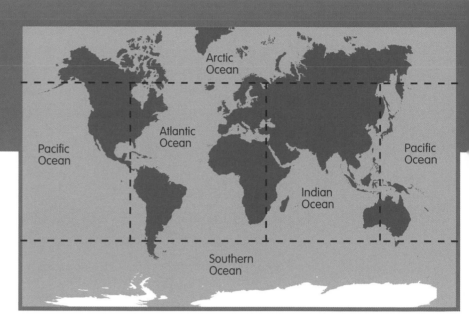

Some people don't think of the water on Earth as broken up into five oceans. They see the water on Earth as one large ocean called the World Ocean.

In some ways, the idea of a World Ocean makes a lot of sense. All the oceans on Earth are connected to one another and when you sail from one to the next, there is usually very little immediate difference between the two oceans. However, the more we study the oceans, the more we learn about their differences.

INDIAN OCEAN

ARCTIC OCEAN

PACIFIC OCEAN

The Indian Ocean is far warmer than the Arctic Ocean, meaning that it can support different forms of life. Ocean currents, like the Gulf Stream, are often contained within one ocean and only effect their surrounding area. As we discover more about the world's oceans, it may be that we find more and more differences between them.

CHANGING EARTH

Global warming is a process that is causing the temperature on Earth to slowly rise. Global warming is caused by harmful gases in Earth's atmosphere that trap heat from the Sun on Earth. We have just explored Earth and looked at the different continents and oceans that cover its surface. However, if global warming continues, then the surface of our planet will not remain the same for long.

If humans do not stop putting chemicals into the air, dumping waste into the oceans and cutting down huge areas of forest, then our planet will soon look very different to how it does now. Global warming could cause the temperature on Earth to rise, the ice around the Earth's poles to melt and sea levels to rise.

If the ice around the poles melts, large areas of land may end up being permanently underwater.

GLOSSARY

bordered   to be next to another country, district or continent

canal   a man-made waterway or river

canyons   deep gorges with rivers flowing through them

civilisations   societies that are very advanced

countries   places that occupy a particular piece of land and are run by a government

cultures   the traditions, ideas and ways of life of groups of people

expeditions   journeys undertaken to explore or research new areas

extinct   a species of animal that is no longer alive

fertile   soil that is able to grow strong, healthy crops

founded   established or originated

indigenous   originating or naturally found in a particular place

islands   areas of land that are surrounded by water

landmass   a large, single body of land

landscapes   visible features of areas of land

magma   molten, liquid rock below or within the Earth's crust

mainland   a large, continuous piece of land that makes up the main part of a district, country or continent

politics   the activities associated with running a country using a government

population   the number of people living in a place

pressure   a continuous physical force exerted on an object, which is caused by something pressing against it

remote   situated far away from main centres of civilisation

species   a group of very similar animals or plants that are capable of producing young together

submarine   a sea-going vehicle that can submerge itself and move underwater

tectonic plates   the pieces of Earth's crust that move around, changing the face of the Earth and creating volcanoes, mountains and ocean trenches

INDEX